You & I

Echoes Of Love As Fate Unfolds

Deepti Kenjale Khopkar

BookLeaf Publishing

India | USA | UK

Dedication

Srushti Rao

I am dedicating this book to you. Without your aura and motivation, this work would have remained unfinished. Thank you for your unwavering support and encouragement. You are a true embodiment of the saying, "A glowing woman can help other women glow and still be lit."

Aadish Ashish Khopkar (Pillu)

I fight, endure, and grow for you. You are my source of power and strength.

Kenjale Family – My Pride, My Strength... So Much Love!

Preface

I have built narrative poems to tell a story
that captures the special moments and
struggles a couple faces while striving to
complete their love story amidst various
issues. When one partner gives up, the
other stumbles, facing the world alone. Love
is not a candy to cry for and ask your
parents for it; it is a commitment to
communicate, stand firm, and live by it.
Every life has a love story—some succeed,
others do not. Sometimes it is WE, and
other times, it's
You & I.
I made several attempts to find the right
flow, and I'm glad I was finally able to
complete it.
This is my first book, and I hope you enjoy
it!

Acknowledgements

I acknowledge the pillars of strength in my life - To my Dad, *Ravindra Yashwant Kenjale,* for being a visionary man and empowering me, for giving me the freedom to rise above every challenge; and my Mom, *Jyoti Kenjale,* for being with me and making my life easy (at all phases).

Special thanks to Ashish Khopkar, my hubby, for being my best friend, sincere critic and helping me stay relevant into this ever-evolving world.

To Dr. Deepali, Dr. Deepika, Dnyaneshwari and *Om,* for your constant support, love and respect.

Sohini Maitra, for being my first reader and editor.

Last but not least-

Hanumant Yashwant Kenjale (Papa), I know you are always with us, empowering us.

Miss you!

1. What It Meant?

Strode out of my house three at night
My maa wondering and my dad asleep
Walking the road swallowing darkness at sight
A heavy throat, no tears yet pain running deep
Steps with no thoughts, not sure wrong or right.

Had called a stranger, booked his car
Stood there calling him, but no reach
Uncertain if he would find the roads, or would breach
Flash! Lights drove as I saw a vehicle at far
Sat for a journey, eluding thoughts of pain and scar.

Shunned the torrents of thoughts trying to burst
More of darkness more of poignant
Clinging taut tears to endure the journey moment
Freeing would turn my path astray; worst!
Had just one question- of what it meant?

2. Marriage House...

Sun rose as darkness was fading
Hitherto, optimism in me was nearly dying...
No fear, merely doubt about my action storming
I knew not where, but kept on wading
A last try to stop negative cascading, No hopes albeit!

There I got, not knowing the further way
Dialled his friend, to aid me with my path
To my luck was answered, early for a dawn ray,
Dazed of my step, pal got there to handle the wrath
Stopped at the turn- pointing the way, he too knew the
further was grey...

A vision of the white coloured house with trees surround
Recall of the place, a small house few years around
Embraced it then with no other expectation
Now the place transformed, however didn't seem of any
celebration
Is this the marriage house? I stand, astound...

3. Wish To Be True!

Astound! No one there, I stood two days before;
Staring at the swords on the wall, I knocked at the door,
They would welcome me, hear me and adore
Perhaps he has paved the way, so the house is minus
décor
His marriage called-off, our relation would happily roar!

Few questions, false No, more laughter...
Together, we would face all doubts, now and after.
Few adjustments and find our happily ever after,
With respect and care for each other, hereafter.
No worries to bear, no issues to bother.

My heartbeat raced, a joyful shout;
Travel-fun-play-romance and pose with pout,
Our relation carved a victorious route!
In this December cold, we would sit with coffee-warm
and true.
Happy cue-I wish for this dream to come through...

4. Two Days Before...

Astound! No one there, I stood two days before;
Staring at the swords on the wall, I knocked at the door,
It was wide open, knocked again eyes on the floor,
His mom walked, no greet, evidently a shock to her core.
She seized my hand, pulled me away—what else was in
store?

Tears rolled, as I set myself free,
She questioned my presence, devoid of glee
She thought I came to shatter the marriage, but you see,
I was just there to clear the wrong, I said as I plea;
Not money, no plot of my kin, only love being the key!

Blurry words as I cried sadly,
Unprepared was I, my words unheard- hurting badly!
"His father's prayer nearly done, avert mess get going",
She said, she did not want me any more second staying.
Attempt failed, as my steps were leaving.

5. I Love You, Baccha!

I sat in the car, overwhelmed by tears,
To me, the world felt like it was breaking apart.
Her words remained, refusing to leave my ears,
So much more she said, but I can't bear to write.
For me, falling in love felt like a curse.

Few miles away to highway
Rang my phone, it skipped my beat,
It was his call, the one with whom I was complete!
Within fraction he reached, it was still an early day;
The clear me was uncertain, should we just run away?

Called me to his car, next to his was my seat
In next two days, it would be someone else sitting here
Shattered with pain, realising true would be my fear;
I collapsed into his laps; I cannot stay with you, cried in
repeat...
I Love You Baccha, he whispered as he accelerated,
steering us down the street.

6. Feeling Worst

My car drove behind us; he waved to stop it there.
We drove far on the highway, as my tears did not stop.
Worried, he moved his hand over my cheeks with care
Was this the end, he had given up, was it fair?
Many questions, thoughts, fear started to pop, non-stop.

Tilted my head, cool air flew through the rolled-down
window
It is the end, I said softly, banging myself on the seat
pillow
Drowned in my thoughts, I heard him say Hello!
His mom had called him asking whereabouts.
He remained calm; growing was my anger and doubts...

He lied he was at barber for a haircut,
To look his best for the day, he muttered...
Gazing, she apologized to him for no strut.
Unable to sink-in her words for me
I felt worse for those then the chaotic relation I see...

7. Going With The Flow...

"Are you hungry?" he asked, his voice soft and free
Eyes swollen with tears, too pained to see
Knowingly said yes, wanting him for some more time
with me
These might be our last moments—just wanting to live
free
Sat down at a café, knowing the fate, or changing it if
together we flee.

He insisted on it about it few weeks back
Why would I do wrong to my parents and flee?
Can't things be fine and on track,
Then again, did his parents reject me for my shade was
black?
For them, he told, I was too bold, arrogant, an
unconventional knack.

Staring at him with a bread piece in hand,
Hard to gulp - our dainty affiliation having such an end...
No question on how I reached early or care to show

Devoured his meal, unbothered; unruffled- going with
the flow...
He had accepted, now was my turn to guard my heart
and stow

8. Loving Is Crime...

Dropped me to my car, he turned to embrace goodbye,
Hesitating, I set for the distance with a heavy sigh.
No words spoken, no hopes fulfilled, unmet my beliefs
high
Hardly could he do anything, was known to me
Nevertheless me being I, how can I let situation control
me.

Started my journey back, still the morning time
Shiny sun, silent winds cold, driver playing the sad old
chime
The man in this time must have got the tale's prime
Lost and entwined, crazy all these years was my love
mime
Silly, sorrowful, hurting, was love truly a crime?

Thoughts free now, no longer bound so taut
Nine years would end, tough thought
Pondering across the road, all this real or a reel plot

Scenic passing on the move- Mountains and fields
Sobbing with every breathe, unlocking emotional shields

9. Love Is In The Air

The sweet times, when love meant we,
The mild breeze, soft music, and two bodies' one soul we
see.
Tiny hearts entwined, that aura all around,
Joyful and free, where no logic was found.
He is mine, and I am his—our hearts play a timeless
sound.

Evolving smile curving from speech till ears
Rising the cheeks glowing and pink
The breathless lungs when each nears
The blush, the love and tangy wink
The naïve stage is so nascent, far from any fears

The brushing of hands, the gentle touch of fingers,
A first glance exchanged, a promise that lingers,
The first embrace, the first blush, the first kiss,
The moment! Heartbeat seems amiss.
It's a commitment, and I am solely His.

10. Love

A year or more, we chatting and being together,
As friends, to be comfortable rather.
Relationship started blooming and enhancing;
Sitting together at his office one evening,
An unbreakable connection was unfolding.

Tugging me closer, wrapping his arms
So close, two hearts beating, for each, in left and in right!
Realisation of us being one; the nascent charms
Darkness fainted and the eve was bright,
We breathing of each other as he holds me tight...

Entwined fingers sealing salient promises
United we stand, even if the world bridles
Expressing- Only the truth, however harsh.
In addition, no empty words of moon and stars!
Enduring together hindering fights and wars.

11. Moonlight!

Not ever made me wait, upright there before
Being shield from rain and sun at the shore
Ate from one plate wherever we went,
Time was good! Together we spent...
Love and life, perfect to the core!

No gifting, that was our mutual rule,
No compromising our work and school;
Not crossing any limits, maturity – the only tool!
Trust, Care, Respect being the foundation,
Fights too weak, resilient was our relation.

Care and love he showered,
He said, "Can wait for you for hours unbothered"
Drove miles to meet me – dining desk flowered,
Raising the bar, against everything the love towered.
Together lively were two souls, perfectly aligned!

12. The Waves...

Visionary me engrossed into studies and career,
Not ever wanted the bond to be a barrier.
His support held me sane on my path;
Away, he moved remote, brave for his parents world,
hath!
Anxiety, restlessness engorging wrath!

Strong we held tight in the storm,
Managed ourselves as per the new regime.
Maturity holding breath, we met in months unlike norm!
Talks reduced, chats vanished as the days went by,
Long-distance, living in the memories, with faith in time,
sigh!

It did not cease us- we were stronger,
Although meeting at times but were longer...
Years went by, we into each other, smiling deep
Moments sufficed until the next leap.
Loved each other, moon and back, vowed until the last
sleep!

13. The Tides

A firm and resolute 'NO' it came,
Would there be help? We were still figuring the same.
Sitting at Marine Drive, he felt the weight,
His family's conservatism, he spoke with a sense of fate.
I stayed hopeful, with positivity in every word I spoke.

Storming mind stressed and stuck
His mom knowing our story had rejected
Telling him, "Your dad will never agree". No Luck!
Struggled to find a path, strongly affected.
Seemed as the road ended, no future reflected...

Mature enough to know our decisions,
Seemed someone is taking the right of us...
Ordering of a decision, devoid of any discussion;
He assured of finding a route out of the fuss
Life would be fine and together, as just!

14. His Love Won't Lie!

Born nine months and nine days before my own day,
I was destined for him, a beautiful bond array.
Dreaming of perfect life through countless nights
Certain we'd triumph, no matter the fights or flights.
Destiny won't have alternate play!

Stayed calm as the year slipped by,
My parents still unaware, not the right time!
Both busy, relying on time to get things align.
Doubted myself for giving up, with worried cry
Trusted him, definite enough, his love won't lie!

My kins and friends advised, we were not a good pair
I was outspoken wheatish, he reserved and fair,
For me I knew him well, and like his name was unique
and rare!
Trusted my capabilities to carve my path, to earn my
living,
All I desired was him by my side, having our lives
thriving.

15. Out of Blue!

Inseparable, he touched my soul,
I was with him against all odd poll.
Whatever it is, our relation wasn't wrong, maturely led
Met on a weekend to clear the air,
Essential; to decide the path ahead

Petite was meet, the things going havoc
Naive, no answers for the fear in me,
Families seek a groom for me, scenes going tragic
Certainly, we had to create a path, route through it, else
no magic!
No words loosened, as the time passed, weird choking
static.

Fleeting condition, met guys one after another,
New reasons to reject and time to search other
Some rejected me, many I had to
Time to give my parents a cue...
Shocked, this was coming out of the blue!

16. Heartening

Unexpected, my dad had questions
My answer to each- "trust me"!
"I would manage, live it as that's the commitment by
me..."
"I assure of not leading it to any regressions"
Accepted to meet him once, albeit, many expressions.

Too many creases in a chapter he had,
Yet, just for me, for my love, agreed my Dad!
"He trusted me and my decisions", he said.
A ray of hope was evolving,
Everything now would turn fine, heartening!

Seems like a movie scene, but was real
His Paa rejected, stating for me he was not ideal!
My Dad had no points to place,
Astonished! How can one's own father create his son's
negative base?
Still hopeful, though our love story was far from the
race!

17. Don't Know Why

Enough faith in our relationship,
Convincing his parents was his ownership.
He denied me meeting them, not sure why!
His sister, sounded a support, sigh!
Numerous trails tried, only response was deny...

Time was passing, and I should move on
How can I? Not even for my Dad's request.
Kind parents by my side, was in a blessed nest!
Bothered for him, his rapport with his Paa was gone!
Thinking, who would make it right for no wrong?

Sure was I, we would pass his parents test,
For us would be a perfect dawn!
However, his engagement in plans, cracked ribs piercing
heart as I hear the on...
Ahh! The date - my birthdate, auspicious and only day
best;
Rings exchanged, time slipped as grains of sand,
repressed!

18. The Dread…

Everything seemed to cease, added with eruptive fights,
Detached for days, lost in the sorrow of endless nights,
At no time thought, truth hit hard, engaged!
Did he move on? Was it easy? Emotions tangled,
enraged…
Wanted to choke myself, world seemed caged.

He would be silenced, gulping his tears
For his words were unheard, they fell on deaf ears,
For where he lived, was all alone
Burdened by responsibilities, the only son!
I asked thou to talk, seek the happiness he deserves and
desires.

The date of marriage announced,
Six months later, the invite read…
Stood for hours on many days to meet his parents, for
the verdicts they led;
Never supported by him, step renounced,

Always keeping his word, paced away without meeting,
as he carried some dread!

19. Wish I Could Restore!

Ten years rewound as I travelled back,
Resting my head on the window rack
Tear drops caught by wind drifting away.
Life is capricious, learnt my way,
Shattered me hard, leaving my heart with irreparable
crack!

Not a movie, with story ending at theatre exit
Cry loudly; shout badly- the ongoing feeling...
I heard of love's triumphs, but mine was failing!
Alone, through the traffic heavy heart sailing...
People were right- I had not commit!

Off the car, boarded a train,
Noon was not sharp; hair tossed in the wind as I stood
by the door...
No choice but to absorb it and further sustain,
Sobbed more by Mumbai's marine shore,
Wished, had more time for relationship, possibly to
restore!

20. Blaming My Fate

Trusted assurance of being together we,
Blind in belief, blocked by horizon, for me to see.
Take me there-he did not allow me alone to cross the
roads;
Now, leaving me on my own as my life implodes...
Nothing settles the agony, feelings ablaze free.

End is just good in movies and real is rare
Given times to agree, the life is so unfair
Sharp cutting, as it is about love and care
Life, ahh! Rest battles are easy to fight
Conversely, these ones stab deep, no easy or light.

Every inch of my body hurting,
With no food, both mind and flesh weakening,
For all the stress, over weeks had lost hair and weight,
Looking underfed, no glow, blaming my fate...
Quizzical if was off beam or believed a wrong mate

21. The Long day...

Snoozed after I reached home, thirteen-hours travel!
Alone, battled on all fronts, leaving me there-he
surrendered, growing gravel...
Wide eyes open as I sat awake, seemed like a dream
The dawn travel- ten years journey collapsing, aching
extreme!
Stunned on the day passed by, coveted to cry and
scream...

Lost was my world, I believed nothing,
Somehow wanted the scenario to turn bluffing!
The world was full of heartbreaks; I was added to it,
Everyone just lives by it, accepting the split!
To me, how can I? Helpless was I, thoughts kneading.

The day was ending, so was our relation,
To the dust was my trust, lied the equation....
Just a day in between, I had the invitation.
He was far, much beyond my reach, bang!
Tears dried, everything drifted! My phone rang.........

www.ingramcontent.com/pod-product-compliance
Lightning Source LLC
La Vergne TN
LVHW021345200726
843509LV00014B/2675